WEDGES

MAKE A POINT

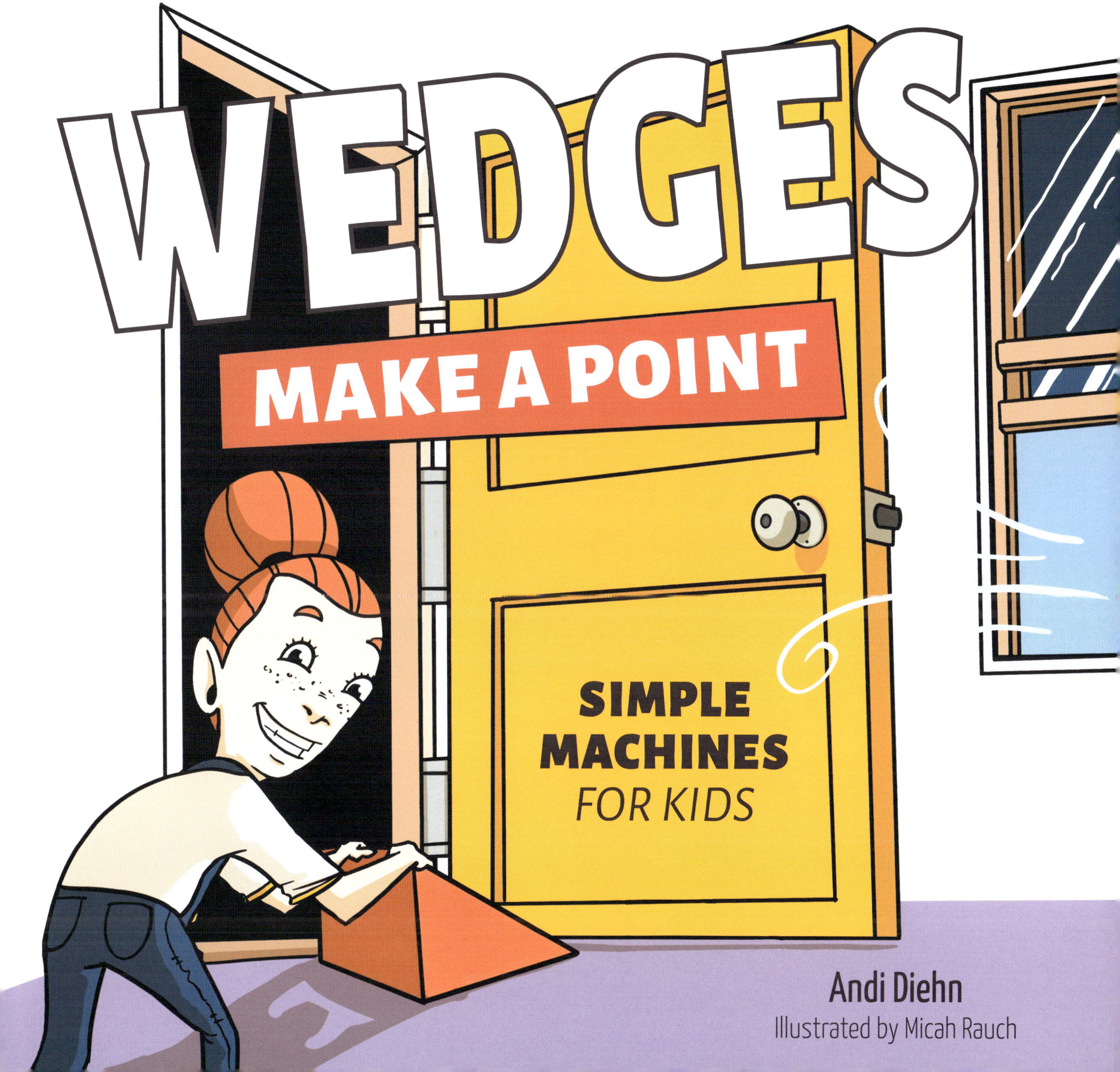

SIMPLE MACHINES
FOR KIDS

Andi Diehn
Illustrated by Micah Rauch

EXPLORE THE BIOMES IN THIS PICTURE BOOK SCIENCE SET!

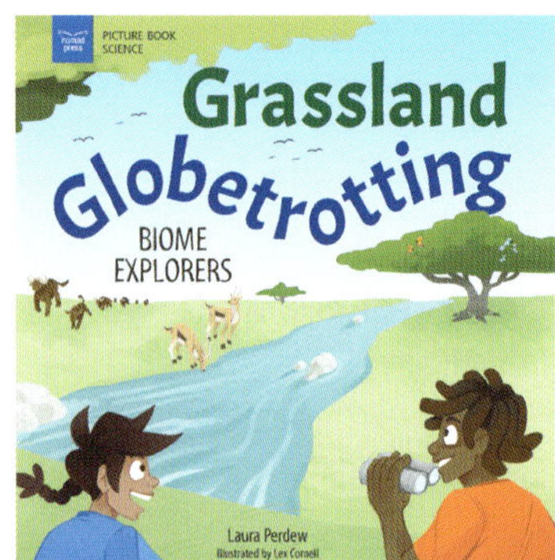

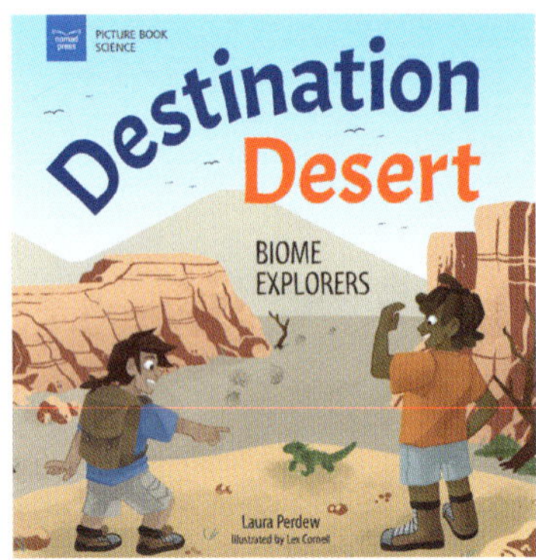

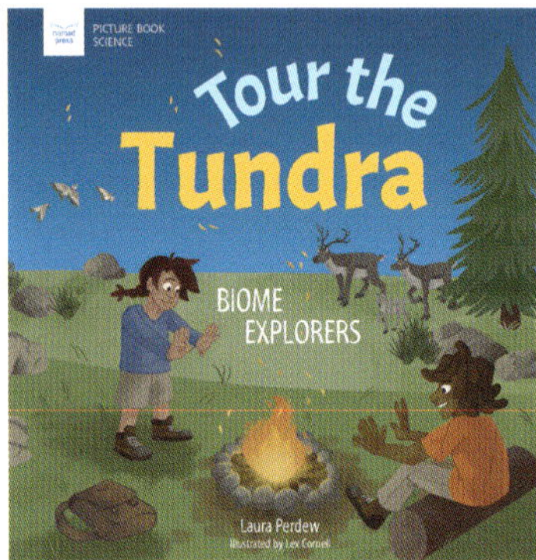

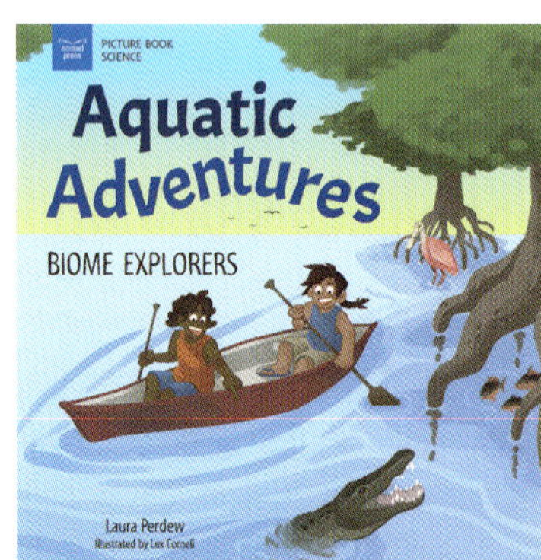

Check out more titles at www.nomadpress.net

Nomad Press

A division of Nomad Communications

10 9 8 7 6 5 4 3 2 1

This book was manufactured by CGB Printers,
North Mankato, Minnesota, United States
November 2023, Job #1066645

ISBN Softcover: 978-1-64741-106-0
ISBN Hardcover: 978-1-64741-103-9

Educational Consultant, Marla Conn

Questions regarding the ordering of this book should be addressed to
Nomad Press
PO Box 1036, Norwich, VT 05055
www.nomadpress.net

Printed in the United States.

Dogs might obey when
you tell them to "Stay!"

But doors? They just don't listen.

To get a door to stay, wedge
a wedge against the door
and rely on friction!

Ice cream might be easy
to scoop with a spoon,

But not chicken nuggets!

For that, you'll need a
wedge—a knife!

Have you ever tried to keep a door open by placing a **bowling ball** in front of it?

Did it work?

SLAM!
Probably NOT!

Bowling balls are **heavy**, but they ***roll.*** Your door would **SLAM SHUT!**

What you need is a **simple machine**:

A **WEDGE!**

All simple machines work because they give you a **mechanical advantage.**

A mechanical advantage makes your pushing and pulling force much more powerful than when you use only your own muscles.

A wedge is a device shaped like a triangle that has a **THICK EDGE** and a THIN EDGE.

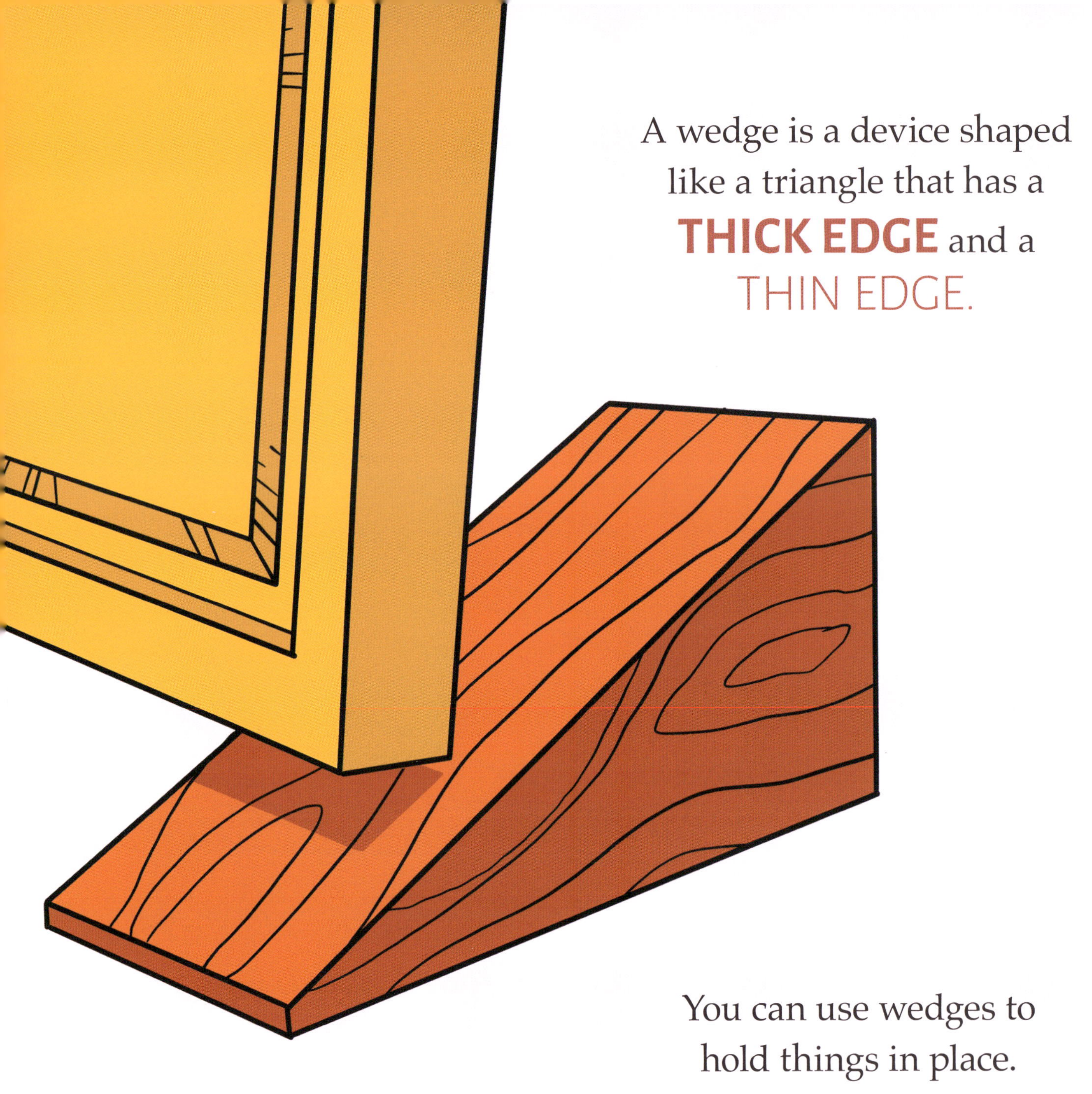

You can use wedges to hold things in place.

A wedge works perfectly to hold a door open! This kind of wedge is called a **doorstop**.

You can also use wedges to
BREAK things **apart.**

An **ax** is a wedge that you use to split wood.

A **shovel** is a wedge that lets
you dig and move soil.

How does a
wedge work?

All simple machines change the **DIRECTION** or the **STRENGTH** of a force.

A wedge transfers force from *one side* of its shape *to the other.*

Picture the doorstop.

The THIN EDGE of the wedge goes under the door.

The **BOTTOM** of the doorstop is against the floor.

When force from the door ***PUSHES*** on the doorstop, that force is ***moved*** to the side on the floor.

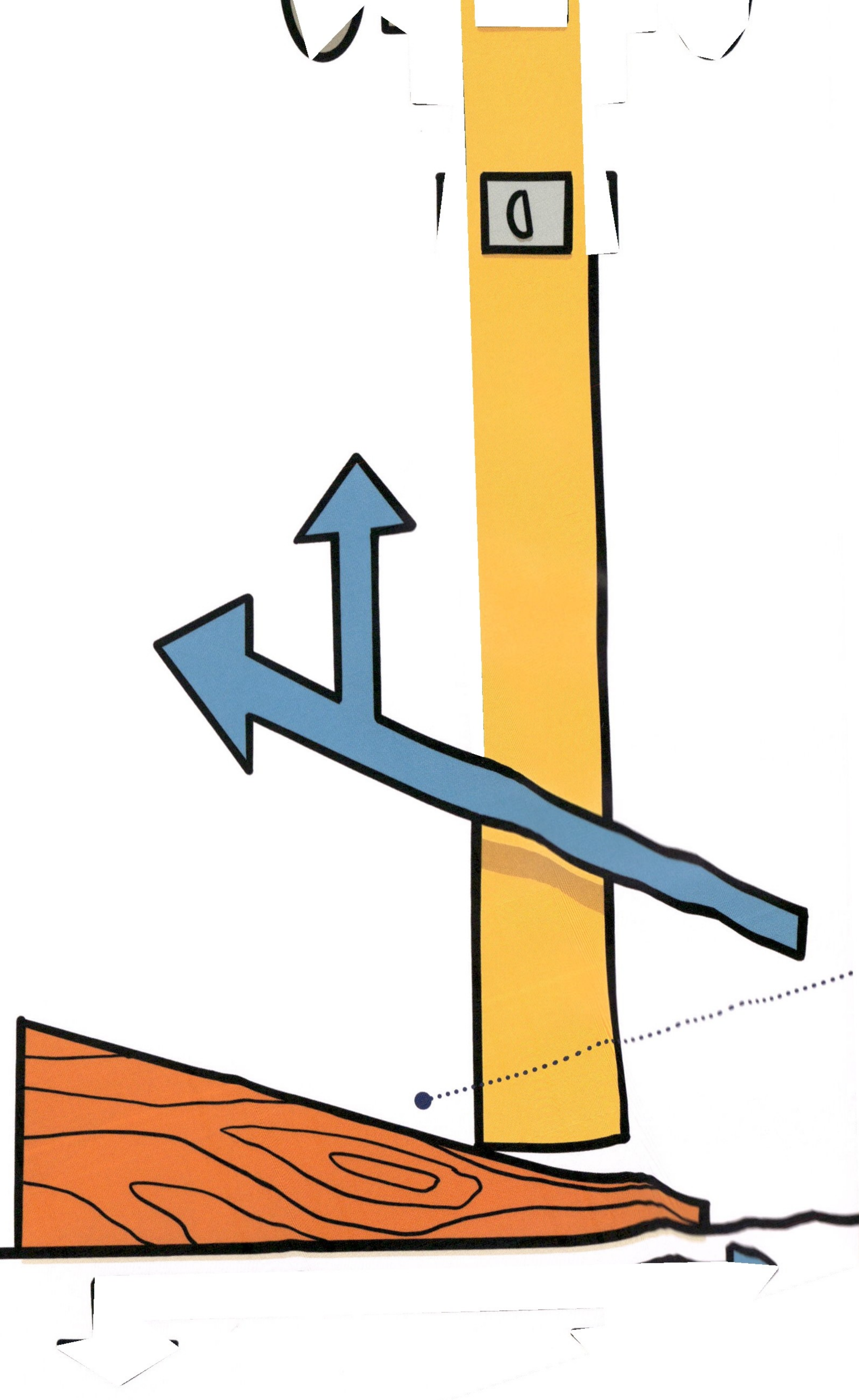

Rub your hands together. What do you feel? That heat between your hands comes from friction! When two surfaces move against each other, that creates friction.

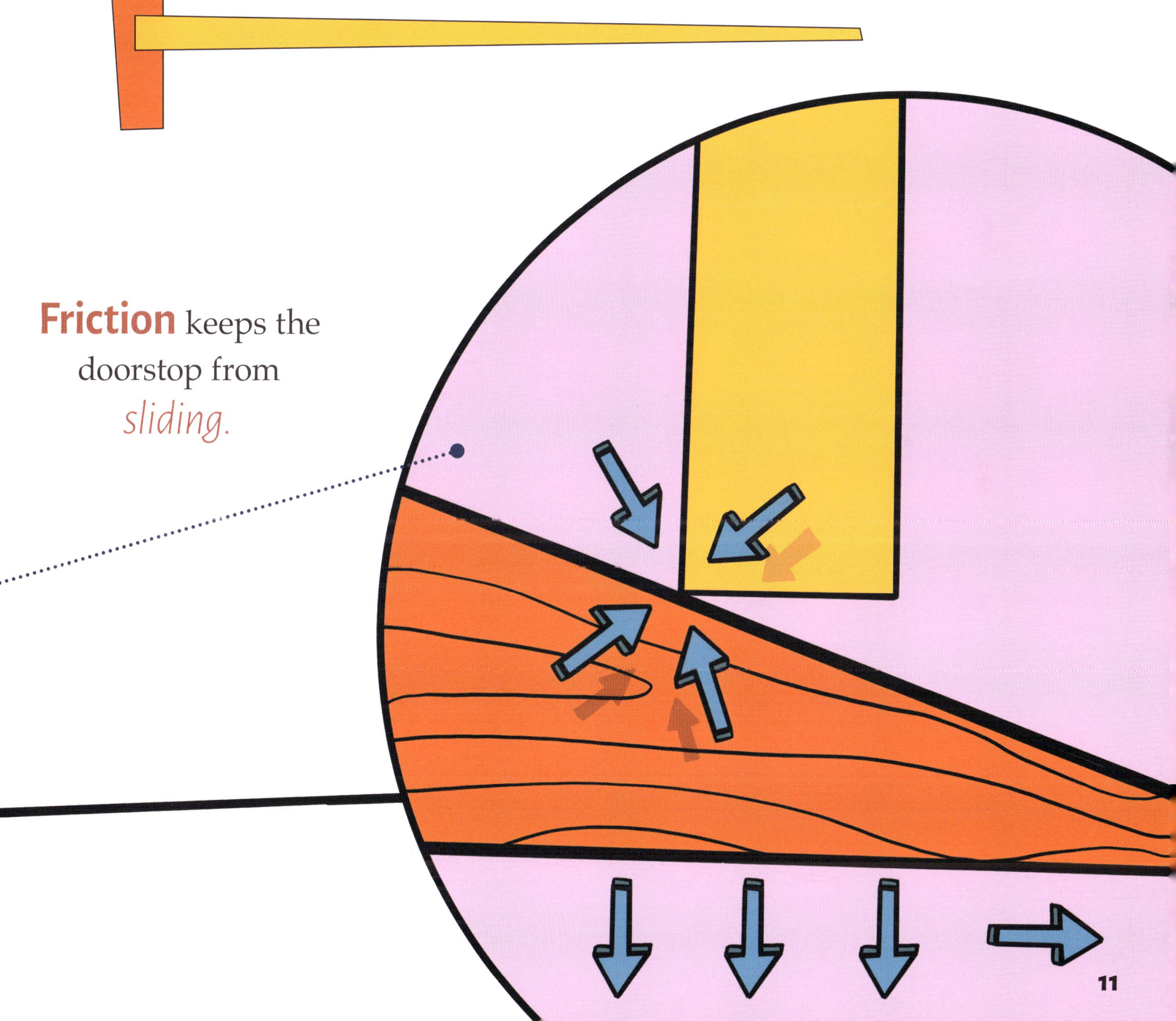

Friction keeps the doorstop from *sliding.*

A **larger** form of a doorstop, called a **wheel stop**, can be stuck under the wheel of a truck to keep that truck **from rolling away.**

The **friction** of the wheel stop against the ground keeps it from *moving*.

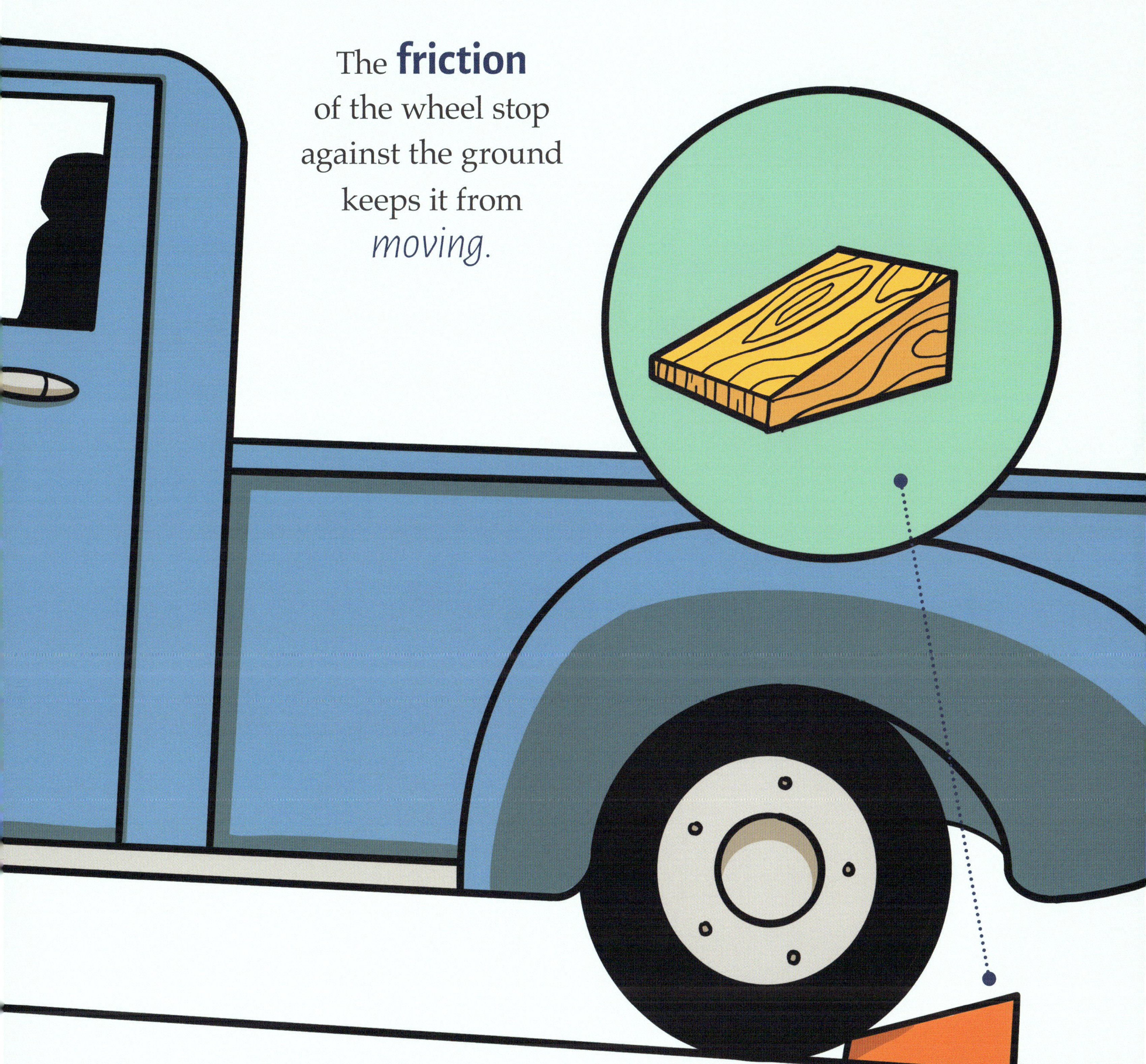

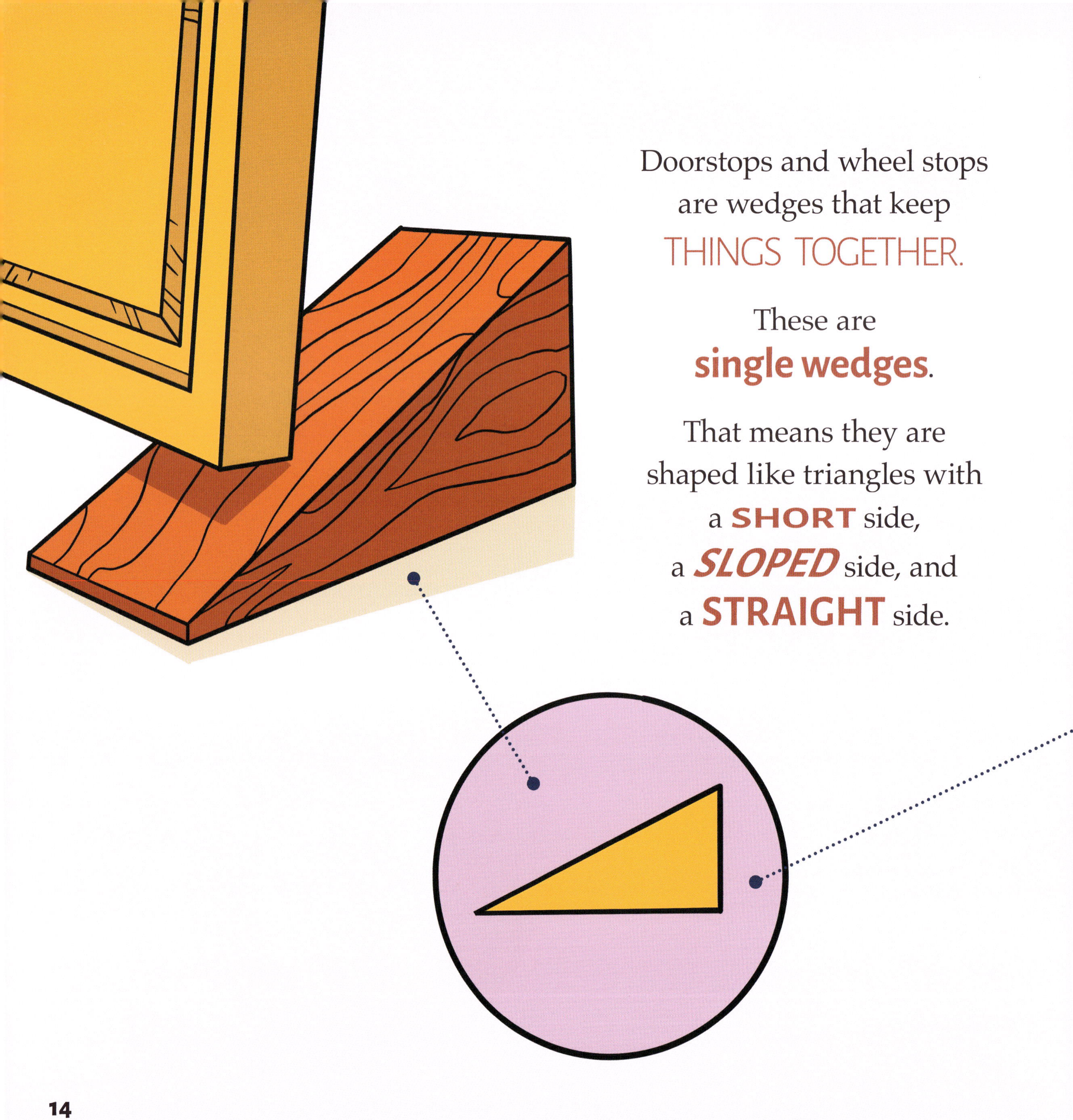

Doorstops and wheel stops are wedges that keep THINGS TOGETHER.

These are **single wedges**.

That means they are shaped like triangles with a **SHORT** side, a ***SLOPED*** side, and a **STRAIGHT** side.

Sometimes, people think of a wedge as a moveable inclined plane. An inclined plane is another kind of simple machine. A ramp is an inclined plane.

A **double wedge** is two single wedges put together.

Double wedges have a **SHORT** side and two ***SLOPED*** sides that come together—no straight sides.

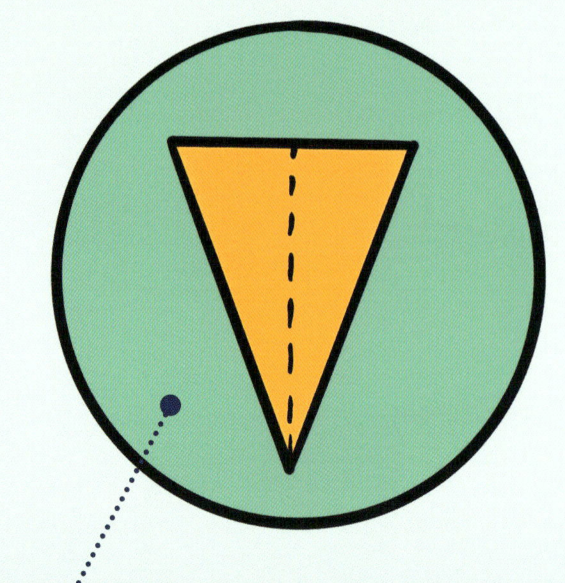

Can you imagine the head of an ax?

That's a double wedge!

Double wedges are great for **breaking things apart** instead of holding things together.

Would you cut your steak with a spoon?

NO!

Instead, we use knives to cut steak and other foods. And guess what?

A **knife** is another kind of **wedge!**

Look at a knife. **Be careful!**
Ask an adult for help!

What do you notice?

One side is
THIN AND SHARP,
and the other side is
THICK AND BLUNT.

That's a wedge!

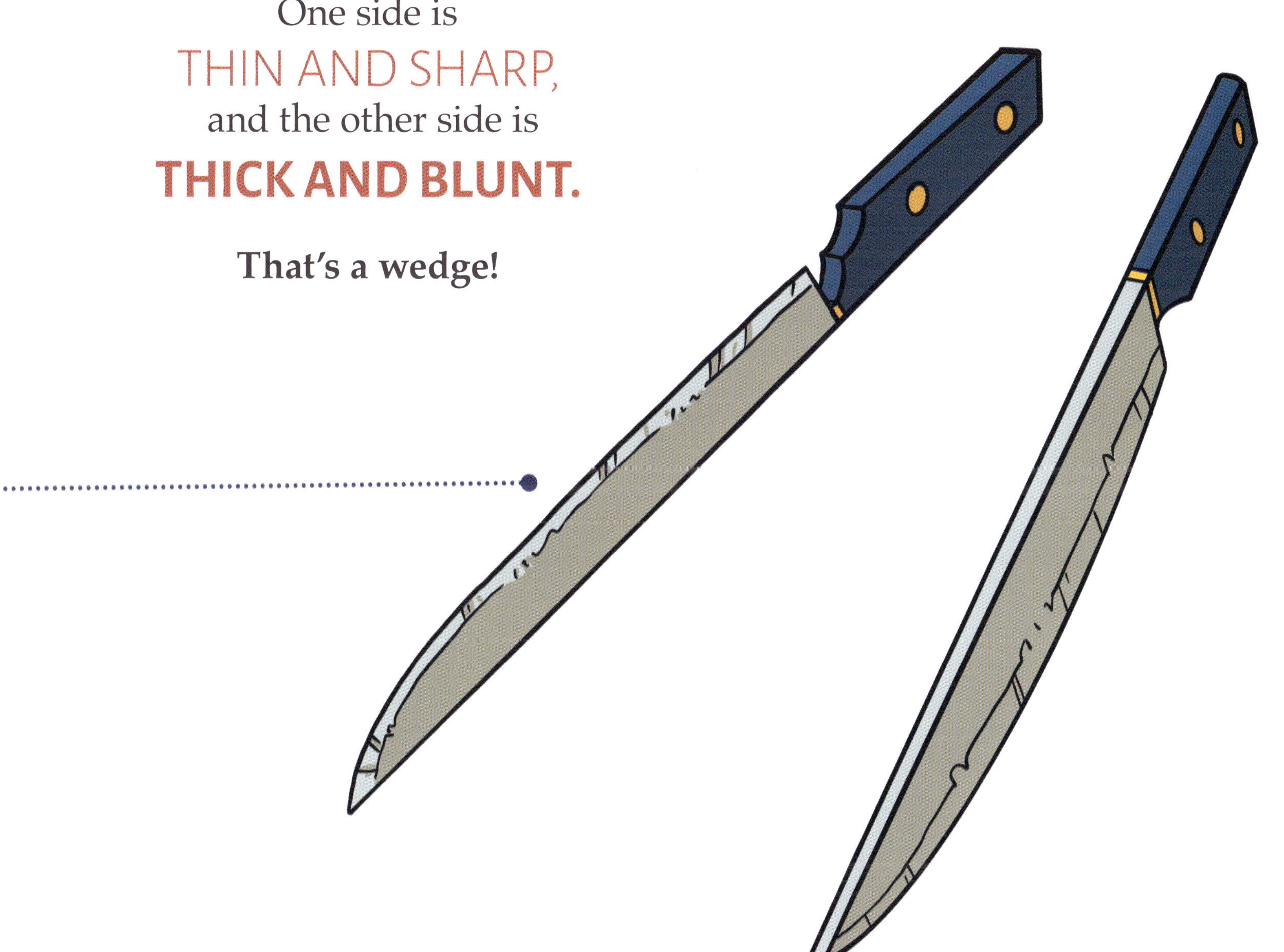

When you push a knife into a piece of steak, that thin part is cutting just a TINY SLIVER.

But as the knife ***MOVES THROUGH*** the food, that sliver gets **BIGGER** and **BIGGER.**

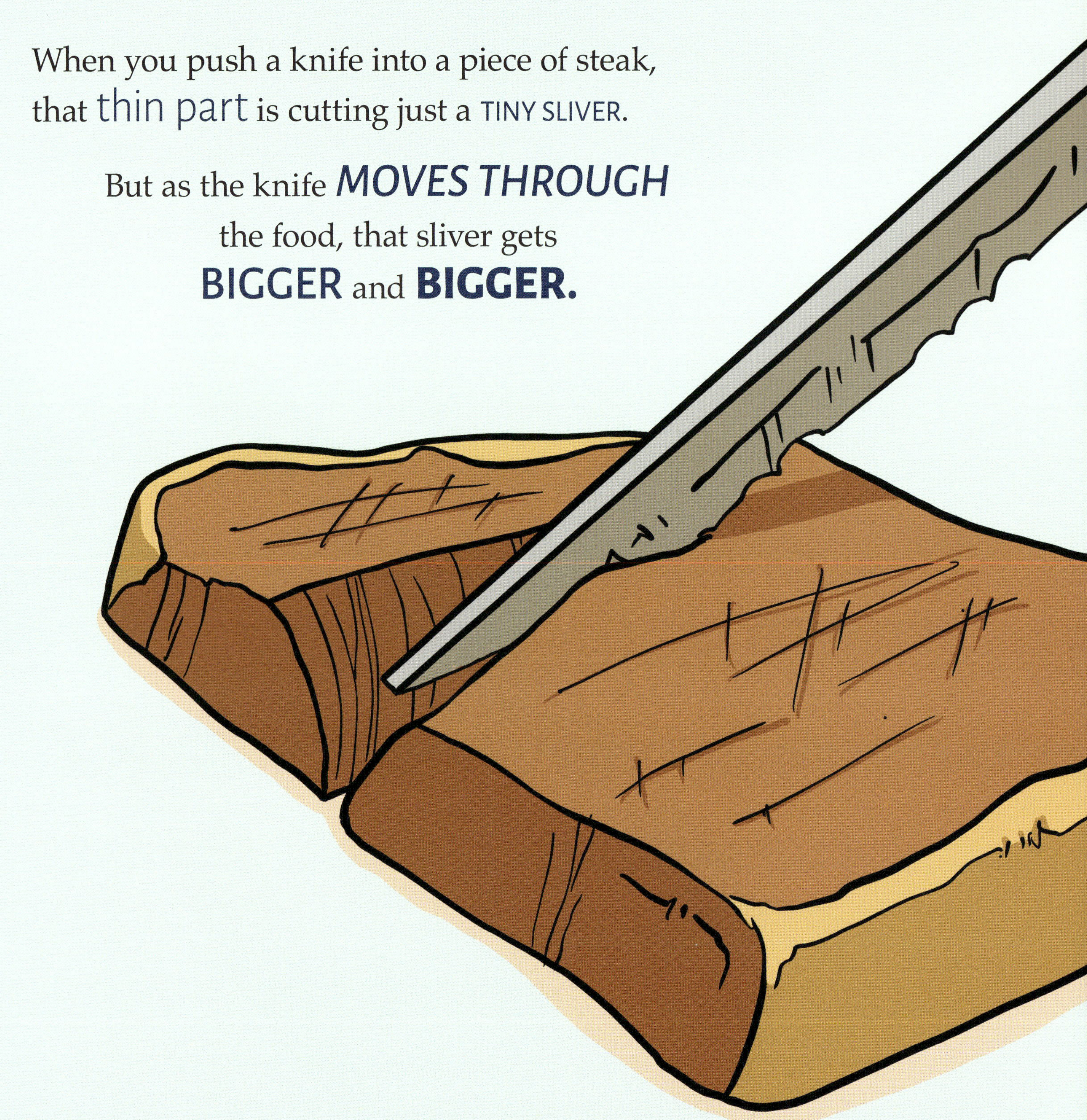

You are putting **force** on the wedge by pushing down on the knife.

That force is **squeezing** out against the steak and ***pushing it away*** from the knife on both sides.

And then—you've got a small bite, easy to fit in your mouth!

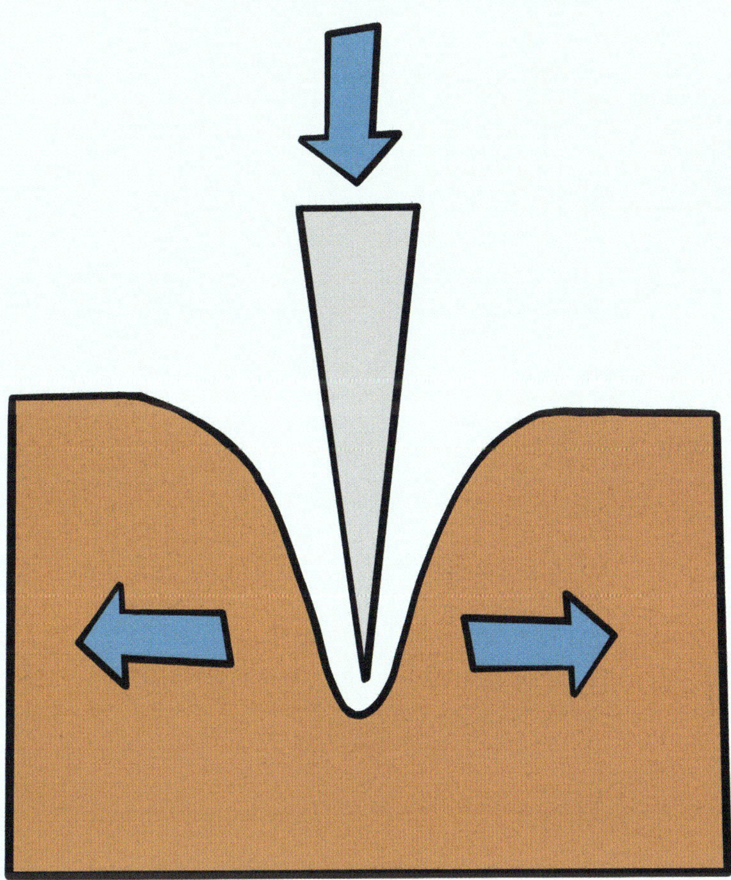

Wedges have been used for many **thousands of years.**

The earliest wedges were probably **axes** made of **stone**.

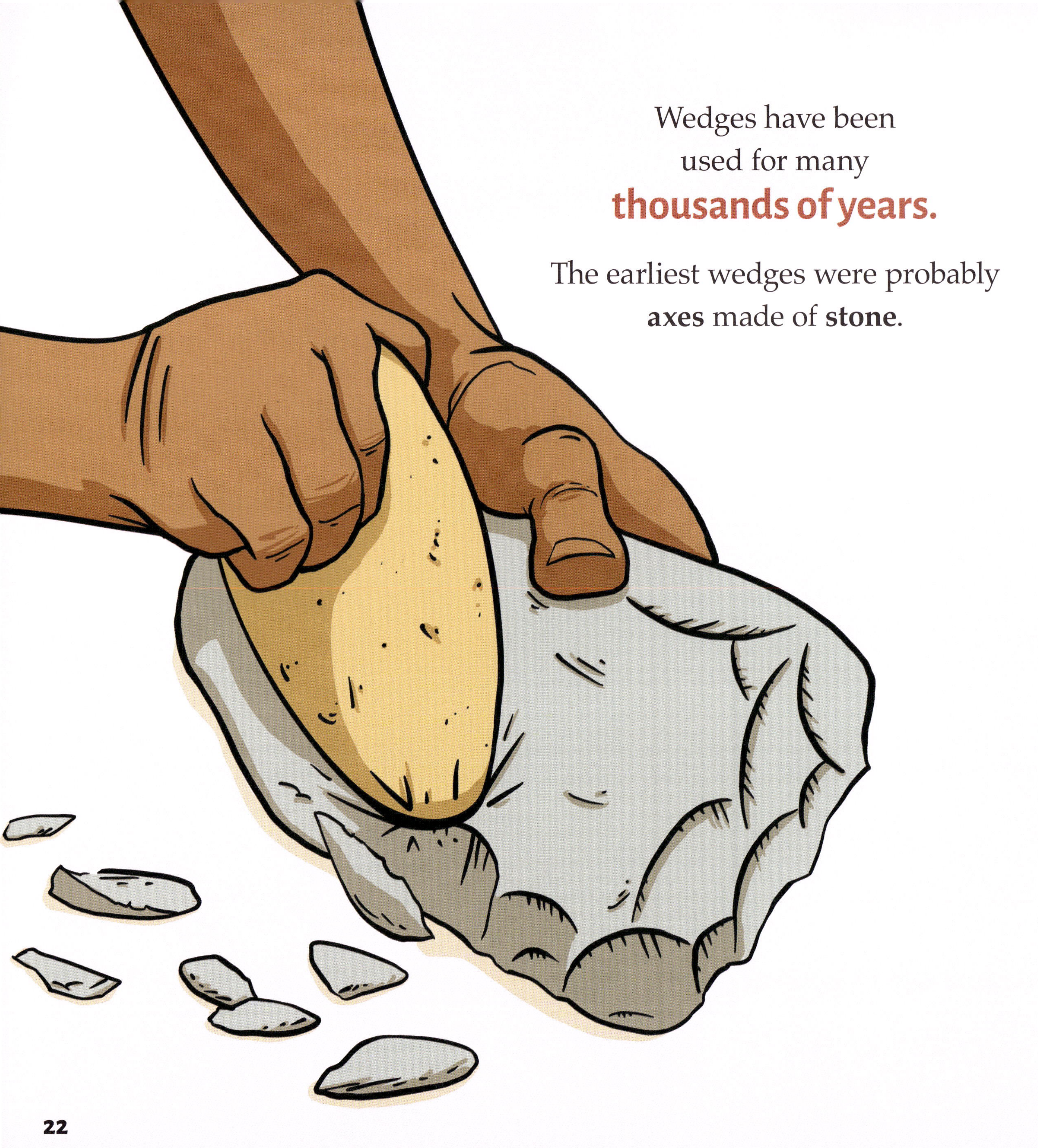

Ancient people chipped away at rocks to form triangle shapes they could then use to cut up meat or split wood.

Later, people got the idea to add a **handle** to make the ax easier to use.

Ancient Egyptians used wedges to cut stones for **monuments**, **temples**, and even the **great pyramids!**

Some of the wedges they used were **wooden**. Ancient Egyptians stuck **wooden wedges** into holes they made in stone and then poured water over them.

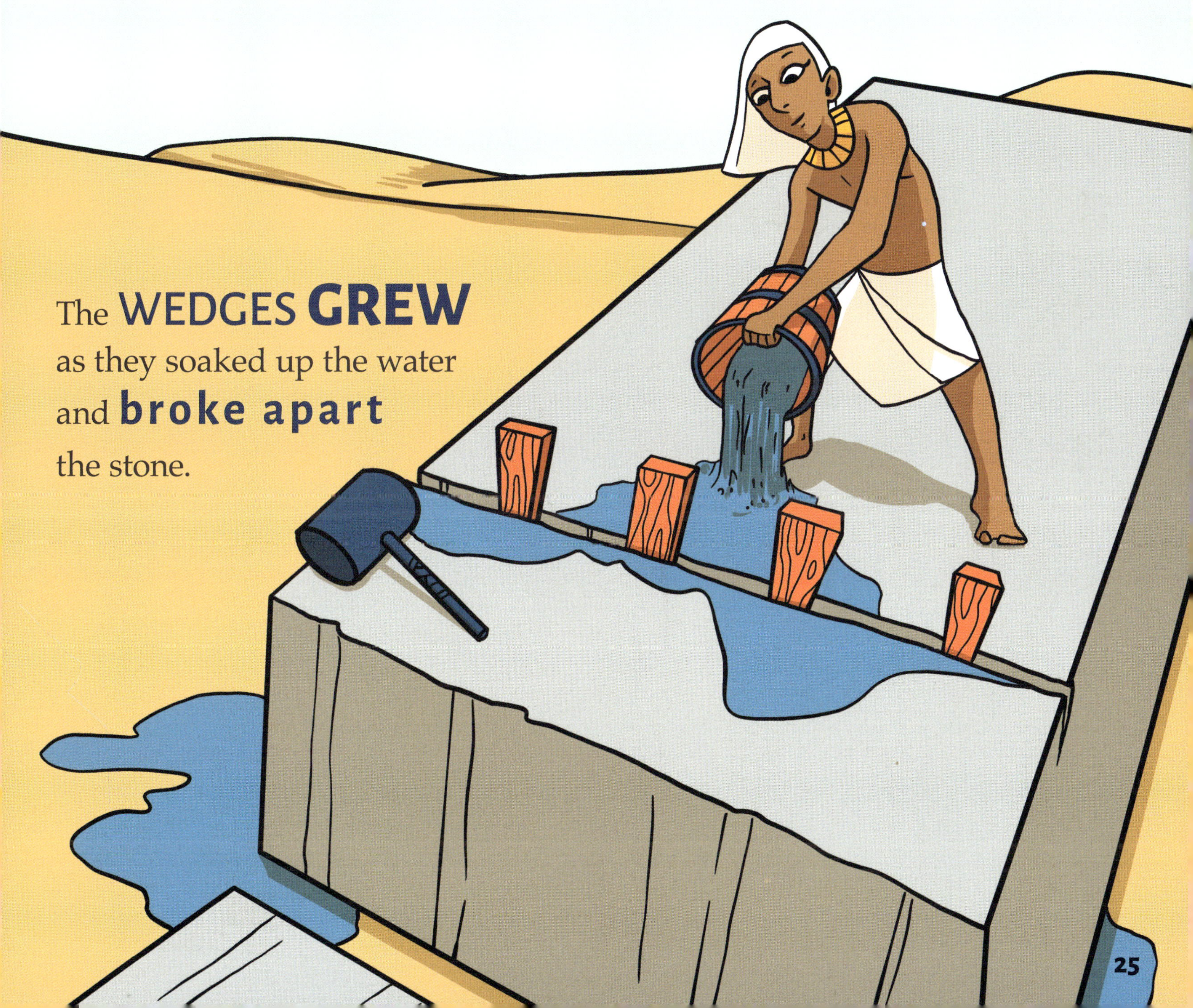

The WEDGES **GREW** as they soaked up the water and **broke apart** the stone.

Some wedges do two jobs—they can push things apart and pull things together. Screws and staples have wedges that can do both!

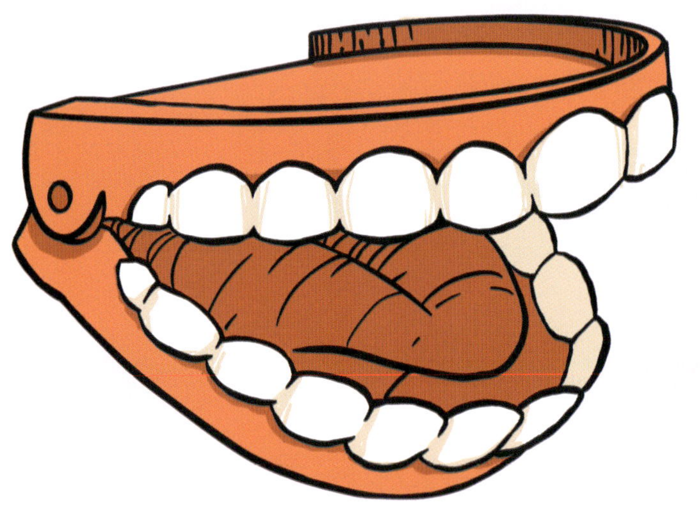

What other kinds of wedges can you think of?

Scissors

Nails

Teeth

Staples

Pushpins

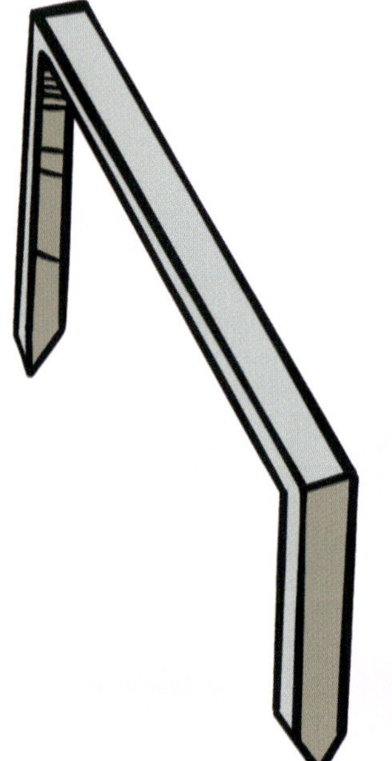

Look around your **house, school,** and **neighborhood.**

Where else can you find wedges? What jobs are they doing?

Activity Time!

CAUTION
Always have an adult help with knives!

Cut It Out!

What You Need

playdough - plastic knife

What You Do

- Roll your playdough into a ball and set it on the table.

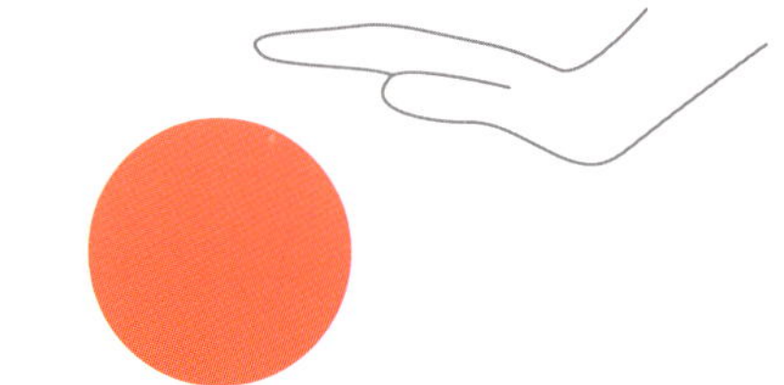

- Try to cut it in half using a flat hand. What happens?

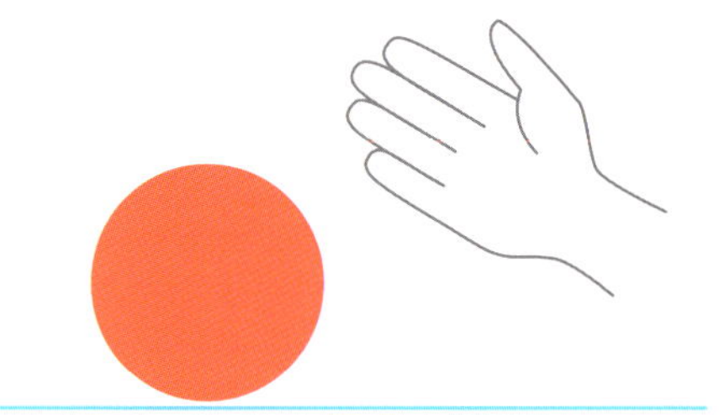

- Try cutting it in half using the side of your hand. Are you able to cut it?
- Try cutting it using the plastic knife. Is this easier?

What happened?

Which tool (flat hand, side of hand, or knife) worked best? Why?

Glossary

double wedge: a wedge that has two sides sloping toward each other, coming together in a point.

force: a push or pull that changes an object's motion.

friction: a force that slows objects when they rub against each other.

inclined plane: a sloped surface that connects a lower level to a higher level.

lever: a bar that rests on a support and lifts or moves things.

load: an applied force or weight.

mechanical advantage: the amount a machine increases or changes a force to make a task easier.

pulley: a wheel with a grooved rim that a rope or chain is pulled through to help lift a load.

ramp: a sloping surface.

screw: an inclined plane wrapped around a central axis used to lift objects or hold things together.

simple machine: a device that changes the direction or strength of a force. The six simple machines are the inclined plane, lever, pulley, screw, wedge, and wheel and axle.

single wedge: a wedge that has two sides that make a 90-degree angle, with one side sloping between them to form a point.

wedge: a simple machine that is thick at one end and narrow at the other. It is used for splitting, tightening, and securing objects.

wheel and axle: a wheel with a rod that turn together to lift and move loads.

work: the force applied to an object to move it across a distance.

Inclined Plane

Lever

SIMPLE MACHINES

Screw

Wheel and Axle